Spiritual Warfare: What You Need to Know About Overcoming Adversity

Dan Desmarques

Published by 22 Lions Bookstore, 2019.

Table of Contents

Copyright Page 1

About the Publisher 3

Introduction 5

Why is Demonic Possession Widespread? 7

How Does Demonic Possession Begin? 9

How does the Devil Gaslights You? 11

How Can the Devil Destroy a Religion? 13

The Favorite Weapon of the Devil 15

How to Overcome You Spiritual Struggles 19

How to Confront Your Spiritual Problems 23

How to Win in Life with Faith 25

How Lust Corrupts the Soul 29

The Importance of Trust in Love 31

Can We Change Others? 33

Why is Introspection so Important? 35

How to Choose Your Friends 37

Can We Change the Physical World? 39

Is Selfishness Necessary for Happiness? 41

How to Evolve as a Spiritual Being 45

Why God Despises the Majority 47

How to Embrace the Holy Truth 49

How to Love Your Enemies	53
The Infantile Mind of Most Adults	59
How to Protect Your Soul	63
The Deception in Atheism	65
The Importance of Prayer	67
The Prayer of the Cross	69
The Prayer of the Pentagram	71
The Prayer to the God of the Invisible World	73
The Prayer of the Chakras	75
The Prayer of Hope	77
The Prayer of Good Fortune	79
The Prayer for Exorcism	81
The Prayer for Soul Liberation	83
The Prayer of St. Michael	85

Copyright Page

Spiritual Warfare: What You Need to Know About Overcoming Adversity

By Dan Desmarques

Copyright © Dan Desmarques, 2019 (1st Ed.). All Rights Reserved.

Published by 22 Lions Bookstore and Publishing House

About the Publisher

About the 22 Lions Bookstore:

www.22Lions.com

Facebook.com/22Lions

Twitter.com/22lionsbookshop

Instagram.com/22lionsbookshop

Pinterest.com/22lionsbookshop

Introduction

Many of us go through life not knowing how to change ourselves, and much less face adversity with a renewed set of values. It may take years to even realize that we have a spiritual problem to solve. And still, when that moment comes, most can't find the answers they seek in any religious congregation.

Our spiritual battles tend to be more devastating and hurtful than any others, and the increasing consumption of antidepressants, as well as the rapidly increasing number of suicides in the world tell us exactly that. As a matter of fact, it is in countries with the highest suicide rates that this spiritual war becomes so obvious, for various reasons that this book explains in detail.

Due to lack of sufficient knowledge on how to handle spiritual confrontations, most of us tend to face repetitive problems, and even succumb into self-abasement. This occurs because we were taught the wrong things by our parents and school teachers, many times even by our priests and spiritual leaders, while being led into believing that the social values we grew up with were correct. And well, they are not. But as adults we can't face that anymore, as it makes us rethink our true nature, question our entire existence, and while forcing us to rediscover our true self.

The work, and the consequences of its results, even if positive, is immense. And this is why most people don't want to change, even when knowing that they need to, including when seeing themselves self-destroy their own life.

We then wonder why those around us don't change, when we see in them things that require an urgent shift of attitude; and yet, we rarely look at ourselves to ask why we can't or won't change. And along this path, we go through life complaining about others and not looking at our real self, our identity and the core of our heart, all of what makes us humans of a spiritual nature.

That, obviously, demands a deep introspection and a confrontation in front of the mirror of truth. And the vast majority of the population, either doesn't want to do that, or doesn't possess the necessary weapons to withstand the turmoil that unravels within during those very dark moments. Instead of that, most choose to wear a mask of goodness, and here we find another spiritual trap in which the vast majority falls easily.

We can only overcome such states of mind by looking at what we are doing with our life and with ourselves, and before we can even recognize the deep web of complexities we are in. Only afterwards, can we start seeking for answers that make any sense, and lead to effective results. And if you have reached this stage so far in your life, this book is surely for you, for it will guide you towards the values and rules that make people want to change, while explaining how such changes are made.

This is not just a book about how to change yourself, help others, or face a spiritual warfare, but also a book that will give you the full spectrum of what changes are, and while explaining why most people always change, quite often, for worse.

With this in mind, it is hoped that this compilation of information can guide you towards your most desired dreams, and despite the paradigms of the masses which are destined only to entrap you.

Why is Demonic Possession Widespread?

The world is rapidly changing, and creating three divisions among people. These divisions are precisely and interestingly portrayed in many apocalyptical movies. One group, the masses, represents the living dead, the braindead, the zombies, reacting on impulse and completely unaware of what they do or why. It is as Jesus said, when dying on the cross: "They do now know what they do" (Luke 23:34).

These individuals are being moved around, pulled and pushed, against their will, or under their will, if we consider they have no conscience whatsoever, or even a sufficient amount of empathy to justify any.

They tend to think that it is all within their will, and so, when feeling this energy within them, in their heart, they cannot process an explanation for it. As they are non-human, or pre-human, they have to process the transformations within their mind; and in doing so, they find a reason for it outside of themselves.

Very often, the reason found for their emotion is the opposite of what would be logical to assume — they attack the innocent, the passive, the kind, in search for a scapegoat to blame for their misfortunes.

But why are the innocent attacked? Well, the answer is that, basically, they cannot or do not want to defend themselves. That's why they make the perfect victims; for they create the ideal scapegoat; I.e., they are, or willingly become, what others seek.

Many are the reasons that turn people evil, perfectly described in psychiatry as a form of psychopathy, and in religion as demonic possession. Whatsoever is the case, or the perspective adopted, all paths turn towards the same end when we look at narcissism, or more precisely, Narcissistic Personality Disorder.

Not only all characteristics are parallel to psychopathy and spiritual possession, but also in line with what the bible tells us about the last days on earth: "People will be lovers of themselves, lovers of money, boastful, proud, abusive, disobedient, ungrateful, unholy, without love, unforgiving, slanderous, without self-control, brutal, and not lovers of the good, but treacherous, rash, conceited, lovers of pleasure rather than lovers of God" (Timothy 3:1).

This is indeed in accordance with the way society is transforming itself. It is now known that Narcissism is not just a mental disease of the minority, but a mental illness on the rise, quickly spreading to the whole of humanity. And few know, through parallels between religion and psychiatry, that Narcissism is just a new found scientific word to describe demonic possession; or in other words, demonic possession is on the rise. It is expanding very fast. And when I was investigating why it is so, for the past two decades, I found a bridge between two worlds — mental and spiritual — which creates a vacuum, an open space for demons to take possession of an individual.

This space is created by ignorance. Reason why Jesus said:

"My people are destroyed for lack of knowledge; and since they have forgotten the law of their God, I also will forget them" (Hosea 4:6).

How Does Demonic Possession Begin?

Evil spirits whisper. They do not have direct control over a soul unless allowed.

The permission, as the process of spiritual possession, is gradual, and comes through the conceiving of small but consistent spiritual exchanges along time. It might start as a simple lie, a robbery of small proportions, until it becomes the slander of an innocent, the deliberate manipulation of a group of people, or even the family of the narcissist; and then becomes the submission to others alike, the abuse of alcohol, consumption of drugs, and promiscuous activities. At this point, completely immersed on the pleasures of the flesh and the mind, the Narcissist, learns, as a vampire, to draw energy from others, by feeding on their suffering - he or she learns to enjoy the pain of other people. And it is here, in this moment, that the demonic possession is completed.

A person literally becomes evil when he or she depends on the enjoyment of evil activities and the entertainment of evil thoughts to feel alive - when becoming one with the demon within. Once this stage begins, the Narcissist can't ever again be alone with himself or herself, and, under the control of the host, begins a quest for blood on humanity.

Obviously, as a predator, his most sought victims are the most innocent, the most vulnerable and the naive. Therefore, this social vampire learns to use his best attributes, both physical and mental, for constant seduction, while studying the vulnerabilities of the most desired prey.

As such, the preferred method comes in the form of sexual alluring, manipulation and the preying on the victim's needs and weaknesses. For they need to be invited in, and these three methods are the physical doors to the mind and energy supply of their targets. "They do evil for the same reason a drug addict does drugs: because it makes them feel good. Hurting and degrading others affects them like a pain killer they get high on" (Kathleen Krajco).

It is not a coincidence that such vampires are usually atheists, for religion and moral has nothing that resembles their mindset.

Nonetheless, many will disguise themselves as moralists by hiding inside religious groups, for here they have an abundance of, if not victims, energy supply and an open training ground. There's no better place to practice mind control, than on congregations filled with those who blindly trust anyone inside their group. And so, you will find the greatest abundance of vampires on Christian and Muslim congregations.

As the number of spiritually possessed individuals, or vampires, increases, we will also continue seeing a growing number of such people, gradually, but consistently, destroying all of humanity.

Worse than that, is to notice that they act in group, and tend to respect only those who are like them. Quite often, they associate themselves in hierarchies, and as such, you'll also find an Alpha Vampire among a group of Vampires, controlling them and telling them what to do and what to think, an individual whom, interestingly, they blindly follow and can die for, or sacrifice anything to, including their own partners and family.

Why they do that? Because they are not humans like the rest of us. "The brain of a predator just does not relate to the living soul of its prey. Watch the behavior, and look into the eyes, of predatory animals while they're making a kill. There's nothing there. They are like machines at that moment. They must be, or they couldn't do it... Humans are animals too and have that same predatory mode. Nature endowed us with it as hunters. It's in everyone. But in narcissists and sociopaths something has gone haywire. They go into this mode against their own kind. And they are permanently in this mode against all their own kind. Because they don't view themselves as of our kind. They think we are here to feed them, just as we think cattle are here to feed us. They can't help it" (Kathleen Krajco).

How does the Devil Gaslights You?

Most people now, triggered and instigated by social media to envy, to desire more, to compete, and to hate, easily accept the demonic whispers that come to their mind as commands for war. And that is how they end up forming an army, a legion of demons.

Moreover, I have noticed another interesting fact in today's world, and that is the unification of minds, the singularity, manifesting between such demonic souls. Because they are everywhere. So just imagine someone suffering from spiritual possession, having friends who are also possessed, and seeing a therapist and a priest who are also possessed, spending time chatting with parents who are also possessed, and not understanding, during the whole time, how everything just feels wrong, completely wrong, and yet, is unified like a mantra by the outside world.

The interesting factor here, is sight. They are all blind sighted to the demonic influences around them and within them. This, because they lack knowledge, experience, and awareness on the topic. And so, like puppets who do not know they are puppets, they're played by the hands of their masters, whom they often can't even recognize. Especially if they are atheists without any faith in the supernatural and spirituality.

The most impressive thing that I have noticed in those who are possessed by demons, is their complete disdain and disregard for the concept of soul, spirit, and even God. They are drunk by their ego and their physiological desires, for pleasure, in the form of sex, power, reputation and recognition. They are obsessed with the fabrication and thickness of their social masks. And in doing so, they forget themselves to embrace their mask as the new self; except that such mask is not their new self, but the symbiotic organism that they have now embraced by freewill - the low energy malevolent spirit that they've accepted within. Because that is what envy, hatred and egotism attracts by the same frequency it emits from within the core of the heart.

Our thoughts control our emotions, and our emotions determine the frequency we shift our aura with, which will in its turn, attract likewise frequencies, thoughts and experiences. But not all thoughts are ours, for our mind is basically just a temple, in which the thoughts of humanity, its subconscious nature, and the world of spirit, combine to form a whole.

In this temple, our decisions are master to everything that flows within. What we accept as a rule, becomes judge over our temple, and its precepts will command our future actions and thoughts, fortifying our ego along the way, and transforming our nature accordingly.

Opposing this massive transformation is a fearful segregation of small groups, often religious. They have taken their beliefs to a high new level, as if edifying the greatest walls they could around them. They are now, foremost, cults, terrorized by the outside world. And, as what you would see metaphorically represented in apocalyptical movies, they live within mental walls, so high, that nobody can penetrate them. Their defenses are thick, and come in the form of endless questions, intended to justify keeping strangers outside their barriers, rather than allowing them in. We are now glimpsing into Mad Max, the Matrix, World War Z, The Book of Eli, Resident Evil, and many other movies alike.

What I also find interesting in this parallel, that we all have contributed to manifest — through decades of Hollywood's brainwashing propaganda, feeding our subconscious mind since our childhood — is that in every single religious group, they have their own Judas too. And just like in those movies, such Judas has the perfect mask; they walk easily among everyone, with an aura of sanctity in them, many times talking to their congregation, and in doing so, throwing at everyone more dust, through their own words, so that nobody can see what is going on behind their back.

How Can the Devil Destroy a Religion?

The Judas of a religious congregation, corrupt the mind of the group, through fear, perverse suggestions, and the promotion of a sense of arrogance.

They shift the values of the group from love and respect to hatred, hypocrisy, discrimination and disdain. And so the enemy strikes from within. And like a parasite, corrupts first the mind of one, then another, and soon after, a whole group, which eventually perishes like any infested biological organism.

Whenever such individuals are present, most members start first suffering with depression, then financial problems, unemployment, and eventually resentment towards one another. Once they start attacking each other and quitting the congregation, the enemy wins.

This process is gradual, occurring through a shift in the energy field of the congregation, but can be seen everywhere, in any religious or spiritual group. And interestingly, whenever the source is identified, the members of the congregation tend to go into denial.

Whenever I identified such person, I was the one who then got insulted and seen with suspicion, despite being received at first as a very moral and spiritual individual and presented to everyone as such.

"The great majority of people just go along with the herd. No matter what it's doing. Because most people's behavior conforms to whatever wins them approval and acceptance among their neighbors in the herd, a cynic can use this power over them to make them build him a pyramid or to march them off to war. But he puts it to most effective use when he uses it to sic them like a pack of hounds on some person or group. That demonstrates his absolute power over them and makes an example of what happens to anyone he sicks them on, establishing for him a Reign of Terror" (Kathleen Krajco).

The greatest demonstration of such state of terror, is seen when religious congregations literally refuse to talk about evil and demonic possession, and you can see fear in their eyes when addressing the topic.

On the other hand, it doesn't come as a surprise knowing that I was always quickly identified as a threat by such vampires. For they are the ones who will come to me with a smile, presenting themselves with their awkward and very deceitful personal questions. They know that I can see them, and they are quick to act in destroying my reputation by creating plausible doubts in the group once I arrive. For "everybody knows that when somebody defends himself from accusations with accusations, the crowd always believes the one who accused first and views the defendant as the attacker. This is irrational, because the initial accuser is the attacker and there is no more reason to believe one party than the other. So, people don't do this in good faith. Indeed, the more preposterous the initial accuser's accusations, the more firmly people believe them. They do this out of self-interest, because the return allegations make them look bad for eagerly swallowing the first accuser's preposterous and juicy lies whole. All con artists are thus protected by the pride of those they con" (Kathleen Krajco).

When I leave such groups to themselves, after the problem has been clarified and identified, they move into a darker state, for they have now committed the ultime sin, i.e., the sin of pride.

They have allowed themselves to be morally raped in the name of egotism.

Let us not forget that, in the metaphorical story of Adam and Eve, "Eve wasn't honestly fooled; she just liked serpent's version of the world better, because it made her able to be as God. Adam's reason for swallowing the lie was even worse: he just did it to agree with Eve. In other words, to please her, he prostituted his mind to her. And thus political correctness was born" (Kathleen Krajco).

This is why all religious individuals can easily be fooled and controlled by the strategies of evil: First, they misrepresent themselves in order to be seen as holy; and afterwards, they sell themselves to a lie in order to regain a pride that was never theirs to begin with, falling prey to their ego.

In other words, the Devil tricks them by preying on their insecurity and fears, while offering an unholy gift, like the prohibited fruit of Eden.

The Favorite Weapon of the Devil

As in movies portraying the end of mankind, we also find a few heroes within our social systems — survivors. They walk alone, for lack of better options.

The food these survivors can find in this wild world, comes in the form of books that enlighten them and in doing so, guide them to the promised land — found within themselves.

The authors of such books, like rebel radio stations, continually spread the message that guides those who can follow it — those who are tuned in to this highly evolved frequency. Because, you see, you need to be already at a high moral state in order to perceive the message when finding it. Otherwise, you don't.

This is another interesting thing that I have found among the lost souls, for they read the books that will maintain them lost and confused, and they follow the ideologies and the practices that will drive them further downwards, towards insanity, they take the antidepressants that damage their capacity to properly think for themselves and see reality as it is, they consult with the gurus that instigate in them the idea of perfection and arrogance, stripping them from any remains of love that may still be left within their heart, and they adopt an ideology of false positivity, which, as a matter of fact, rejects self-analysis and introspection, therefore reinforcing the narcissistic paradigm that makes it easier for a demon to take hold of their soul.

That is what occurs when you deny your own consciousness — you allow another force to take control over it, and in doing so, over you as a person. You literally and voluntarily give your soul away, in exchange for what? A moment of illusory peace? The idea of perfection? The illusion of self-righteousness?

You see, people are literally, through various means, exchanging their souls for demonic powers to have influence on them. They do this through a method of push-pull, in which from one side, they receive the pressure from the outside world, through attacks, insults and depression, and in another side, they get the whispers and promises of a better outcome, through lunatic ideologies that ask them to allow themselves to have their spirit raped, in the name of a better life, one in which all this craziness will be easy to handle.

This is the same promise that all liars make, when pushing their victims towards degradation: "Degrade yourself a little more and I will give you what you want."

That, obviously, as any case in which women are kidnapped and forced into prostitution with the promise of one day be set free, never happens, and there is no better explanation to why, as in the form of a phrase I heard from one of such possessed souls: "It is your fault if you trust what I say and chose to accept me back."

You cannot blame the devil for tempting you, but yourself for falling prey to temptation. And that's the ultimate trap — guilt. For what is guilt but the outcome of deception, when one willingly accepts to be fooled in the name of his most selfish desires, often awaken through his most profound weaknesses. It is the sense of unworthiness, inferiority, and humiliation, that drives us deep into our worst fears, in which faith and self-love disappear, consumed by them.

When such fears become unbearable, one wishes to commit suicide, and so he or she does exactly that, physically or mentally, when becoming someone else, the antithesis — a strong and confident human. Except that such new persona is not himself, but a mask he or she willingly wears in public, after giving up on the true self, after giving permission to the spirit of a demon to control the soul and guide any conscious actions and thoughts; and so, one becomes a subconscious and alternate manifestation of self; not the true self.

Such individuals, when in therapy, often claim: "I can't believe my memories are nearly all erased, and when I try to go back in time, everything in my mind becomes blank."

The scary part of it is that, such "blank", as they describe it, gradually increases from childhood up to present moment. It's very common, on those perfectly possessed by demons, that they often can't even remember the actions they do in present time.

SPIRITUAL WARFARE

Although they very often deny them, in a process known as gaslighting, which still holds a certain awareness in what regards the lie voluntarily spoken, eventually, they lose the capacity to identify their own reality or remember it as a whole. Their life, at some point, becomes a combination of glimpses of awareness, for they are unconscious most of the time.

As their evil deeds become more permanent, the incapacity to confront them leads them further downwards towards unconsciousness. And so, they typically commit suicide, in an accident they promote on themselves, not uncommonly, bringing other souls along with them.

How to Overcome You Spiritual Struggles

As you can imagine, the vibrations of good and evil increase the polarity between people furthermore. It is then with no wonder, that so many spiritual wars manifest themselves in the form of physical conflicts that deny us the capacity for seeing what is really going on. And yet, the illusions of the material world, are simply justifications the mind creates.

As in apocalyptical movies, salvation is found through survival. Our heroes, know where they can't be, and where they should go, and even though they don't know where the end of the road is, they keep moving forward, changing places, and accepting the pulls that come towards them. Because you may not know where you should be, but you certainly and quickly learn where you can't be anymore.

This, if you may accept it as such, is the message of God, showing you the path. And so, there is no need to accept a state of victimhood, for you are only a victim if you accept such state in your mind first.

If you are under attack by a bunch of lunatics, you should rejoice on the fact that they do so because they see in you the perfect scapegoat — the opposite of their energy frequency.

You should also rejoice on the fact that, if you are targeted by evil, you are blessed by good. And good is God. Therefore, the solution consists in embracing this reality, the differences and the transformations occurring on the planet.

You may pray, read, learn, transform yourself, change your location if you can, let go of old habits, and gain motivation through the opportunities to meet new people like you, walking on the same path. And in doing so, you will find your way towards happiness and spiritual strength, while continuing your journey in a systematic evolution.

All changes in life are transitory. You do not really experience a challenge but a change. Whenever a challenge is presented to you, it signals the need to change. Sometimes you change before the challenge appears to you; other times you change because a challenge has appeared in your life; and yet, some other times, you change because a challenge has occurred in the past.

Now, human beings, are easily trapped by their perceptions — what they see and feel at a given moment. They are not experienced in postponing their emotions, control them in time, or even in seeing such emotions from a bigger scale. Because you see, nothing of what you felt, on a certain day, ten years ago, matters anymore. Right? But it mattered a lot to you back then.

Remember how awful you felt when your parents had fights? Remember how lonely and hopeless sometimes you felt? Remember sometimes thinking that you would never be able to attract love to your life, but end up alone forever? Remember how you once felt penniless and broke, and hopeless? Remember how devastating your first breakup was? Or how you felt when someone you trusted abandoned you and betrayed you? Did you forget all that? Why have you forgotten something so tremendously important to you? Because it was not important, ever. You felt that it was, when it was occurring, but it wasn't and it didn't interfere with your future, except to guide you towards something better and greater.

The same is occurring with your life right now, and everything you worry about losing. Your fears for the future, will at some point vanish into something else.

If you could feel more capable, bigger than your problems, nothing of that would ever matter.

Fear and hope can't occupy the same space, and the more faith you have, the less fear you feel, because faith is something of the future, while fear is always related to the past. We fear when we are connecting our mind with what we saw in others, what we heard and what we felt before. This doesn't mean, however, that what happened to others, or even to you, on a given time, has to happen or will ever happen again.

SPIRITUAL WARFARE

Fears are merely memories and perceptions of pain, emotional or physical, that do not need to have and shouldn't have any effect on your present condition.

How to Confront Your Spiritual Problems

Why do we have problems? Because on planet earth, you grow with your problems. And every time you grow up to a certain point, new problems are attracted to you, and naturally, to match your new spiritual level.

Many others have said that Earth is a prison-planet. And although the reasons why this is true are too many to explain in a single chapter or even a book, the fact is that all, or at least, nearly all souls, on Earth today, have been put here to evolve.

The only way such evolution can occur, is if they are pushed towards it against their will. And especially, if such evolution, when agreed upon, favors them tremendously; reason why you can't be wealthy, unless you follow principles and laws that govern wealth, namely, happiness, self-esteem and moral behavior.

However, you can't make friends with the same principles that make you wealthy, because not all souls can understand values that are intermingled with a high self-esteem and a meaningful existence.

As a matter of fact, the more evolved you are, spiritually and financially, the more uninvolved you will see how the large majority truly is, how deeply and mentally sick the vast majority of the population on Earth is: "When one awakens to the truth, he finds that those he considered similar, that before he considered to be normal people, he finds that they are not normal, but abnormal. But this only happens when one awakens. When one is asleep, he believes to be normal and thinks that everyone else around him is normal too. However, when one awakens, with profound pain he finds himself inside an asylum, in which everyone is insane" (Samael Aun Weor).

Planet Earth is nothing but a virtual school of self-development. The material world is nothing but an illusion put before our eyes, to express our subconscious mind, relative to our many lives and preexistences as souls, in order to force us to heal, improve, and grow. "When we disintegrate the ego, the conscience awakens and the mind becomes normal. And only then we realize that we were in a madhouse, or that we are still in a madhouse" (Samuel Aun Weor).

So why can't you breakup with the person you have right now but know isn't good for you or end toxic friendships and relationships in general? Well, because they provide you company, and you fear loneliness, because in a relationship, you also receive sex, and other forms of validation, either emotional, social or physical; and you don't have the time, energy, confidence and faith in yourself to look for someone else, and restart, because they make you feel part of a society, and you don't like to feel detached and discriminated.

You see, everything, absolutely everything that you weren't able to challenge in yourself before, is then challenged by the outside world. And this world will come to you at the same speed that you try to surpass it.

It is, somehow, a lost battle. But could we win? Yes, we can, when cooperating with the world and learning about its rules, even though there are two worlds within one: the world of the spirit and the world conceived by the human mind as a collective.

How to Win in Life with Faith

The message that the bible teaches us, through the words of Jesus himself, is very clear: "Stand firm, and you will win life" (Luke 21:19).

In order to stand firm, one must believe that he will be victorious at the end, which is not possible without a complete surrender to God in faith. Such faith comes from a willingness to reach a certain outcome, which we can envision in our mind before seeing it in the material world. Therefore, faith must be accompanied by willingness, persistence, resilience and belief.

Most people go through their life without goals, without clearly knowing what they want, with more fears than goals. They are so afraid to lose what they have, that they never take any chance towards the unknown.

You know, they can't leave little billy with grandma, or sell their beloved dog to someone else, or quit the house where they shattered so many tears, or leave their friends behind and make new ones, or quit their car and just walk. They can't quit, because they have invested too much. And the only way they will ever invest on something new and quit their old investments, is if that dream, that goal, is far much bigger than their life right now, much bigger than the present, more extraordinary than life itself; or, as often is the case, if they have nothing else to lose, because life has stripped them of everything already.

Why do you think people watch movies, if not to escape their reality? They feel so oppressed and humiliated, that only superheroes, comedy shows and the overdramatic stories of others can make them forget their own.

Some people feel so hopeless in their life and dramas, that only watching talkshows about the dramas of others can help them feel better. Yes, because it always feels better to know someone else got worse from life, someone else suffers more, someone else died while you are still alive. That awareness, even if negative, feels comfortable for many.

It is so, with amusement, that I hear some people telling me that I am too negative, when I force them to confront their problems and their needs, which otherwise they never will, because they are too weak to evolve. Because, you see, negativity is not in what you get, but in how you handle it.

In reality, the negative ones, are not those who have problems or talk about problems, but those who can't face their problems, don't want to hear about their problems, and are too irresponsible or too stupid to solve their own problems. Such people are constantly attracting more problems and pushing fault to others, which is the same as to say that they are like a sinking ship, throwing its water to the ships around it. They bring other people down, with their stupidity, immaturity and irresponsibility. And one doesn't do much of a favor in helping them, for they are experts in nullifying such help by making themselves look much worse than before.

It is then no coincidence that, after a while, we end up visiting them in a hospital, or ending in a hospital ourselves, because of what they do to us.

Truly negative people, lower your self-esteem, make you mentally weak, and destroy your immune system from within, with anxiety and stress. Because of them, you will end up having more problems at work and in your social environments. Because of them, you will have more diseases, and spend more money on therapists.

Meanwhile, they will gladly smile at others and tell them, behind your back, how sick and useless you are; and what a nice person they are, for tolerating you and your pathetic weaknesses, for being your friend when you have none, and for visiting you in the hospital because of what they did.

I have had more fights with people and more accidents within one year in a relationship with a narcissistic woman than I ever had during my entire life, including my childhood. Not even an accident with a bicycle near a road, that nearly got me killed, after the dumbass narcissist started shouting like the crazy she is, was enough to deserve an apology. Because not even your death, will ever deserve any empathy from a narcissist.

SPIRITUAL WARFARE

On the contrary, it might very well make them smile and feel more confident on their distorted mind and manipulative psychopathic rants.

How Lust Corrupts the Soul

Love is always a trap in which we fall with lust. But as in friendships, our relationships should be based on the qualities we find in others. We shouldn't seek a partner to please us socially or sexually or in any other way that we can visualize.

As a matter of fact, it is because we project too much of our imaginable desires unto another person, that we often get deceived and disappointed.

If you wish to attract good love, you must look within your heart: How does that person make you feel? Is he or she trying to make you feel respected? Happy? At peace? Accepted? Understood? Heard? And more: how does this person react to your weaknesses? Does he or she tries to help you, by not hurting you, or does he or she takes advantage of that to control you and hurt you even more?

You can see how lovable people are by looking at their desire to help you in life or to hurt you. Their motivation will show you their true intentions, for it is either to lift you or to drag you down.

People who are selfish, without empathy, and in need for narcissistic supply, will be as vampires in your life for they have nothing in theirs. Their emptiness is compensated by sucking your attention, your life goals and you capacity to control your life, have self-discipline and do more. They are attracted to your qualities, for they seek to destroy them due to envy. And so, what they admire and hate is the same, leading them to never ever have a normal relationship with anyone.

In fact, they will not only envy you but also criticize your best attributes. They will also take pleasure in humiliating you in public, for that diminishes your value through them, as they get to themselves more value by mirroring yours, i.e., your appearance, your job, your social status and so on.

In order to choose a good partner, you need plenty of time. To do mistakes, is easy and fast. But if you wish to find a good spouse, you will need to cultivate a friendship that may fail at any moment. And it is better to cultivate multiple friendships with the opposite gender to avoid heartbreak and also to show your social worth.

For those who see you being valued by others, while not giving yourself to anyone, will value you more. They will know you are not easy or cheap, or easily fooled, that you have high demand and high requirements; but they will also know that they have to work themselves upwards in order to get you.

This emotional competition works both to your advantage and in their advantage as well, for they become better persons for you, as they will be for anyone else, and even themselves; as there's nothing more seductive than a human being continually improving himself or herself, morally, intellectually, socially and emotionally, becoming more mature and also more responsible towards oneself, as well as others.

In your case, it is a way to groom your future spouse before even starting a relationship. I.e., in the competition to get you, to be ahead of others, they will study you faster, understand your needs, and try to be the best they can, therefore avoiding all future disagreements, which are so common to partners who do not know themselves so well. This allows you to start a healthy relationship from the very beginning, one based on harmony, common agreements and common goals — a true partnership.

Meanwhile, those who sought to get you to use you, will see that they have to work too much on their manipulative tactics, and leave your sight soon enough before you have to suffer in the revelation of their true self.

The Importance of Trust in Love

If you can trust entirely in a partner, and you will, once you find the right one, if you have selected him or her among many, you will have a relationship from which love can easily grow, for it is rooted on trust and commitment. From that point on, you can get wealthy, build a healthy family and proceed into growing faster as a human being.

The opposite, a relationship based on physical attraction and sex, is always a relationship doomed to fail, with plenty of spiritual hardships, conflicts and resentment. Simply because it is based on primary needs.

In this case, the chemical unbalance conflicts with the mind, and this leads to the extremes of hate and lust, in the form of extreme selfish desires manifested and projected from one unto another.

It is in these situations that the Devil can interfere to destroy two persons at the same time.

That's why relationships based on lust, which are the majority today, are so chaotic, so passionate and so intense.

We often call these relations true love, and truly believe this to be the case, because they are so dramatic and intense and many movies portray them, reinforcing furthermore this idea. This is the reason why so many people think that they are living what true love should be. And yet, this couldn't be further from the truth, for these relationships are abnormal and unhealthy, and create a spiritual scar, weakening our potential to feel confident in our decisions.

Those who are damaged in such way, tend to seek for further validation, by engaging even more in lustful desires, in sleeping with strangers; and that's why they weaken their own spirit furthermore, until they are completely lost, in the claws of evil.

Such souls, incapable of rest, peace, with endless sleepless nights, end up succumbing even more deeply to the dark energy within them; and these are the women who desperately invite any stranger for a night of sex, just to be able to sleep, to lower the volume of the voices in their head; or the men who pay any amount of money to sleep with prostitutes.

Can We Change Others?

You should not expect a change on someone who cannot yet perceive the need for that change, a person who has not yet discovered her identity or much less the acknowledgment of past mistakes.

How can that happen if such person has not yet suffered any consequences? For as long as an individual has friends, a job, plenty of money in her or his bank account, plenty of alcohol to enjoy, and fun and parties to attend, to rejoice in being who he or she is, and avoid consciousness on the consequences of past deeds and wrong decisions, such person will never change. As a matter of fact, the more conflicts there are in a relationship, the less a person wants to change, when having all that, the more she wants to be herself and reaffirm her position, and the more she will want to party, cheat, and get addicted to drugs or alcohol as a way to escape conflict, at least on a mental basis.

In other words, conflicts reinforce the differences and deny changes.

The only way you can force a person into changing in such cases is by total and complete abandonment. But how can such person change, when abandonment reinforces an even bigger void, that such individual can't live with, and rushes to fill by replacing that same void with the attention of a new partner that she will desperately seek? The emptier someone is, the quicker she is to sleep with someone else. Because she won't be thinking about a long term commitment when desperate to fill a void within her heart.

People who suffer, mentally, emotionally and spiritually, can't have a thinking pattern that focuses on long term decisions or consequences. The whole of their life and behavior patterns is based on a permanent anxiety towards the now. And it is, in the now, that they make all decisions. That is why they seem so immature and irresponsible. They do have life experience and intelligence, and plenty, but only on what regards gratifying immediate wants; and that, obviously, includes experience at manipulation, reading others, gratifying one sexually, escaping the truth, stealing and lying.

When such individuals aren't doing all that, they are either obsessing over social media, gossip or videogames.

Within the desperate need for pleasure and escaping emotional backlashing, people now are so afraid of introspection, that they rapidly find new partners, instead of rather working on current relationships; even their dumb friends will pass the same stupid message unto them: "Forget that! Start again! Find someone else!"

People may seem to repeat the word "forget" like a mantra, as if forgetting emotional connections was as easy as it seems. But what they are actually doing with this mindset is suppressing emotional pain and denying responsibility over themselves — two things which later come back with an emotional impact on their future, leading to even more pain and less awareness — a lower consciousness, seeking to self-destroy itself. And any culture, nation or group which possess the wrong values will promote exactly that through the majority of those who represent it.

Why is Introspection so Important?

Nowadays, the social theory that you should just forget and move on, permeates the whole of society, but denies responsibly and introspection, while promoting promiscuity and depression. And this is why the more people fail, well, the more they will keep on failing. And there is actually more failure in countries where the suicide rates are the highest, because that is what suicide is — self-acknowledgement of failure, even though it's a false acknowledgement most of the times, promoted by a society as a whole, that wishes to destroy anything good entering it or developing from within it.

You only have to look at the values and patterns promoted by such countries to see why that happens.

Lithuania, for example, commonly number one in the world statistics for suicide, is known for having the most promiscuous women, the most competitive society, the highest levels of racism, and the highest level of alcohol consumption and cannabis, apart from discriminating anyone who doesn't look like a local, with constant stares on the street to make anyone feel uncomfortable, and a deliberate hitting of shoulder on shoulder, as you walk pass by them, to make you feel unwelcome.

The levels of aggression, either direct or passive, on any strange element to the country, is such, that I many times questioned myself if the habitants are even human. For they look more like a bunch of zombies from a horror movie.

It is impossible, for any human being that considers himself normal, to enter this country, and after feeling harassed from morning to night with total rudeness, not start hating these people and wishing their complete annihilation from the face of the Earth. Any neighboring country, can immediately make you feel much better with yourself, simply by being there, inside their energy waves.

So what can you do in what regards such people? Let them go and let them fail.

In fact, if you are in a relationship with someone like this, there is nothing else you can do but watch them from a distance and get hurt with how fast they will replace you with someone else that might, much likely, seem inferior to you, in compassion, attractiveness and even empathy.

They are always looking for energy supply. And so, this is a normal reaction and choice for someone who is desperate for not being alone, to avoid the pain of introspection and suffering through the repenting of past decisions.

You do better with yourself by suffering alone and investing on your own changes, by cultivating loneliness. And by this, I don't mean necessarily being alone, but actually socializing, meeting new people, opening your own mental gates to social interactions, making new and better friends. And when the time comes, you may start cultivating possible future spouses. And I say it in plural because you will always get hurt if focusing on one person that most likely will disappoint you.

Then, as you observe them all, and you see them grow, from a stranger into a good lover, you will know them better, from which you can select the healthier and most beautiful flower in your garden of social interactions.

The same principle applies also to your friendships, because most of the people you encounter are not the ones who will be with you when seeing you succeed. Most people are too envious of others to do that. Because the majority of society has a scarcity mindset, and denies admiration to those who have more than them.

The tribalistic viewpoint of the majority, makes them want to associate only with those who are either similar to them, in values and possessions, or those who can offer them something.

How to Choose Your Friends

The best people you will encounter in life don't need much to change, because they have already changed enough to be great friends and companions. They already want to love you. And so, as a team, you will be able to face any future adversity. And those adversities will only make you both stronger.

It is truly a waste of time to argue with a fool, because they will always deny any logic, ignore reason, and basically take pride on your efforts to educate them, as if by doing that, they were positioning themselves higher than you.

There is truly no way you can win in an argument with a fool. That is why they are fools. The stupid can't process themselves out of their stupid mindset, and that's why they are stupid.

Foolish, I would say, would be to expect otherwise, for it is better to isolate such people, and let them be ignored by everyone. This, until society evolves enough to see them as having a severe mental illness, and decides to segregate them into a mental hospital, in which case, Lithuania would probably end up as, not a country, but the biggest psychiatric hospital on Earth.

Such countries, like Lithuania, make the decadence of any nation, during any moment in history, appear, not only normal, but necessary, from an evolutionary standpoint; for what difference does it make, if a rebel army invades a country, when the women of such country prostitute themselves voluntarily and as a priority, to the foreigners visiting it? What difference does it make, if a country was deprived of knowledge for centuries, if when having free access to it, the population joyfully disregards it in favor of their arrogant rants full of imbecility? What difference does it make, if a country has expelled its geniuses and people of culture, if when one enters it, he is treated with contempt, jealousy and hatred? What difference does it make, if a country was deprived from accessing the rest of the world legally, trapped within its borders, if it treats its immigrants with disrespect, unwelcoming starring eyes, and racist remarks?

What difference does it make, seriously speaking, if such country is bombarded to ashes, and disappears from history books as if it has never existed?

Are we all supposed to pay the price for the tremendous ignorance, lack of respect for humanity and uncivilized manners of a few nations on Earth?

I bet many alien races are asking themselves the same question when addressing the problem of human stupidity on Earth. For, every single time, in our entire human history, that one nation was allowed to remain in the dark for too long, it ended up releasing its darkness to the world in the worse form imaginable. And so, it would not surprise me if such nations could, not only support a world war, but promote it and even begin it.

I'm sure that Lithuanians would be dumb enough to pride themselves for being the first European nation to launch a missile on Russia, in the name of North America, and start World War 3. The fact that they take pride on having Nato using their country for military actions shows it.

We should always expect the most imbecile acts from the most imbecile people, and "never underestimate the power of stupid people in large groups" (George Carlin).

Can We Change the Physical World?

The challenge of building a dream life comes from the difference between that dream and reality, the life you live and the life others imagine for you and see as true for you.

Most people would not understand your dreams, and the further they are apart from the reality they perceive for you, the more absurd and lunatic you will seem to them. That's why no great idea ever passed the mental filters of the masses, and what they consider as right or wrong.

As a matter of fact, if most people have very low expectations on you and themselves, they can only process failure in their mind, whenever you talk about your plans to reach something beyond what they conceive as possible.

So how can you reinforce the energy used towards your dream?

Well, first, you can stop talking about it to others because they will suck up the energy from that dream with their negative expectations on you. Then, you can stop giving people reasons to judge you negatively. Yes, conversations are useless when there's nothing to say, but most people don't want to hear about your successes or plans; they want to attach their attention to your failures.

Most people are envious and selfish, and want nothing more than to see others below their capacities, in order to feel better with themselves. And, as so, if you can't talk to them about success, you shouldn't be talking to them about anything else either.

Loneliness is hard to handle, especially in western countries. The world has evolved to such an extent, that we can only find company among the lowers ranks of society, or dream alone, like a lunatic in our lonely apartment or house. And yet, this has been the story of all the successful souls that crossed their reality into higher realms, and built a fortune and a name for all of history to know. Their own years of loneliness, which nobody cares about now, say much more about them than their achievements, because what they had to endure and how they endured it, is in fact, the true reason behind their success.

So how do you endure loneliness, failure, and depression in your path towards success in life?

You don't. You face it. You can't runaway from it. You can only accept it as a part of life. And maybe you need to listen to motivational power metal and epic music every single morning to get out of bed, maybe you need to listen to it before falling asleep, maybe you need to have your headphones all the time with you, and maybe, just maybe, you need to create your own imaginary friends, by collecting speeches from youtube, and listening to them every single day, as if you were talking to that person on the video, interview, podcast, or audio, as if you were all best friends. Because it is better to have imaginary friends talking to you about life and success, instead of having real friends trying to destroy your life and sending you into a deeper abysm of psychological hell.

Most people live in this mental hell every single day, and they feel it deeper when waking up or falling asleep; but it never crosses their mind, that they are themselves feeding this hell by hanging out and associating themselves with the wrong people, for fear of social segregation and discrimination, for fear of loneliness. And so, they exchange their loneliness for a complete violation of their ethics, they exchange friendship with self-worth.

Is Selfishness Necessary for Happiness?

It is a fact that most people in our society behave as parasites. They want someone who can give them something, some nice feeling, some acceptance, some love, but they can't provide any back, and quite often, they don't want to do that either. And the delusion of living with such souls while expecting them to realize it, delays our own development.

Selfishness is not a requirement to be happy, but it is always better when you are selfish next to the right person rather than absorbed in hateful thoughts coming from disrespect and resent emerging from someone who wishes and expects you to fail.

A woman that says: "You don't make enough money" is never better than one who says: "I will do whatever is necessary to make you succeed, so that we can be happy together". And yet, the first is basically a gold digger that deserves nothing from life or anyone, while the second, is so rare, that even imagining her speaking seems like a product of fiction. But, how can a dream be lived, and how can life have hope, without imagination?

It is always a welcoming and pleasant surprise from life when reality shows the possibilities we only dreamt about. But how many times does this need to happen? How many wives or children do you need to have? How many houses do you need to possess? How many Lamborghinis or Ferraris do you need in your life? What do you really need to recognize happiness and its opposite?

You see, if you can process a very good dream, you have already overcome the genetic limitations imposed on you.

Life is so very short that if you count on random events and the years ahead, if you let yourself go with the flow and look at life as a journey without the need for a strong commitment, you are more likely to fail. According to the speed at which the world moves, you would need at least, three hundred years, to learn from experience, fail, adjust your needs and requirements, set new goals, succeed, and then pursue a plan towards your idealistic goals, which you would have redesigned based on past acknowledgments. But that's not what happens, is it? By the time you are forty or fifty, you are finished, without hope, or energy, or ambitions.

In order to maintain your faith, you need to keep visualizing your dreams. Without visualization, there are no dreams. You need to be aware of what you want and ask for it without fears or judgments. Otherwise, how can you possibly get it?

You see, if you don't believe in yourself, you simply won't even put the efforts to match your visions; you won't get the ideas, you won't seek for the people who can help you, and you will not feel,... and pay attention now to what I am telling you: you will not feel what you should be feeling when having it; and therefore, you won't recognize the emotion, the vibration that matches your dream when it approaches you. You will most likely repel it.

That's why people tend to go somewhere and stay, adapting themselves to situations that are "comfortable" and "familiar" to them, while rejecting everything else that feels strange, alienating, and even uncomfortable. But how can you tell the difference between what is alien and what is simply unknown but desirable, unless you can reprogram your mind, to feel what you must know first how it is supposed to feel?

Here is the key to that: You must be able to imagine yourself in your desired outcome, before you get it. And once you do get it, it must feel like *déjà vu* to you. This includes wealth, love, friendships and even the future emotions you wish to experience.

You will never be happy with your life until you can feel happy within yourself first and imagine yourself happy in the future. And for that, you need imagination. The more you struggle with your life, physically, mentally and emotionally, the more dedicated you must be to the act of imagining an alternative reality, the more you will need a quantum leap, which can only occur under the circumstances described.

SPIRITUAL WARFARE

The gap between the inner and outer worlds must be such, that you become independent from the mechanics of the physical world on you, and that means not having the need to react to any situation, no matter how devastating it might seem. Once you can do that, you pass the spiritual test, and as an award from God, you get a quantum leap — an opportunity that you can't refuse, pulling you out of your current reality and into a new one — the one you envisioned.

How to Evolve as a Spiritual Being

Our reality is fundamentally supported by a symbiosis and not a competitive struggle for survival. We all have strengths and weaknesses, and we all get better by learning from one another. That's how evolution was made possible, even though now it seems that evolution has turned into a personal choice.

A very large amount of books out there are merely repeating answers that have been provided for thousands of years. Some pervert the messages, many misguide people, while very few clarify the truth. Even I, by myself, cannot do much, for myself or others. But I have been guided towards many answers and that's what I share with the world. And this, as much as I improve my strategy with the Divine guidance that is bestowed on me.

Every person is a particular case, and should digest my words as it seems fit for his or her situation in particular. And surely enough, many cannot even accept the message, if I do not look like the prophet they imagine. That's why the representations of Jesus and Buddha have more to do with the imaginary of the masses than the truth.

Taking into consideration that Jesus was, very clearly, and according to scripture, an ugly and dark skinned man of grey hair, I doubt that the entirety of the Christians of today would even take him seriously if they met him inside one of their congregations.

I do not see myself as ugly, but I do tend to scare people away, especially when I don't shave my face, and to be confused with a criminal, stopped in any airport I want to pass, either to leave or enter a country, and for "random investigations", as they say, and also accused of being a member of a criminal organization wherever I go, and for whatever reason may justify such foolishness in the mind of those who have nothing better to entertain themselves with, when not being as stupid as they are on a daily basis.

Such craziness can actually be useful when I enter a coffee shop and most people immediately empty it, leaving me with plenty of seats to choose from. Besides that, it is actually amusing to notice that I have always been much closer to becoming a member of the security forces than anything else contrary to it, or that I'm still connected to some of the most important religious organizations in the world, with very strict moral codes and restrictions, which are, actually, constantly supervised. Even the fact that I can publish spiritual books, based on a vast amount of well-kept secrets, had to be approved by them, and was, because of the immense trust they deposit on me, including when asking me for advice on their own work.

I can, furthermore, feel honored for being often invited to participate in private meetings with the most highly ranked members of such organizations, for they've helped me in understanding my true nature faster than I could on my own.

This said, I can only assume that I have an energy, attitude and confidence that scares most humans, and will create a worse effect in the future, as the gap between me and the rest of the world keeps increasing. This would explain, at least, why whenever I enter a shop, in Switzerland, Spain, and many other countries, people tend to look first at my hands to see if I carry a weapon and intend to rob them.

I always see such behaviors on those who are very poor in spirit. And yet, most people who entitle themselves as being spiritual, often have considerations about being "good" which are actually poor and weak representations of humanity, most of then completely detached from the true meaning of life at a universal scale. And I have to admit, that I needed plenty of knowledge to reach a level in which I could judge properly the state of things on Earth, for I was confused during many years of my life, about how to see all this situation.

Interestingly, now I am often blamed for judging, because the stupid masses will always be stupid, and scared of whoever sees them in their real state. And that's why my readers benefit so much from my books, to break free from this sheep-mentality of the majority, that will just and always be representing themselves as they are — a self-destructive section of humanity.

Why God Despises the Majority

This vast majority is despised by God for a vast amount of reasons, and does not deserve life, much less eternal life, which would merely be a perpetual state of decadence for such souls.

They lack the minimum attributes to even be at the state of what could be labeled as human. And this is why acts of love in animals amaze us so much. It is so, because we don't see them among humans anymore, not as often as we see them in mammals or even reptiles.

It then becomes obvious, for all the reasons mentioned above, that you will find in my writings a stage of spirituality that appears far above all religions on Earth, for it is intended to connect you to the highest realms, the ones which vibrate with the life of other planets, and towards which you must ascend, if you truly desire to continue evolving as a spiritual being. And nevertheless, by the description of my own life experience, it should be clear as well, that you won't get to that level without paying the ultimate price, for you will be hated and persecuted by the vast majority, among which you can include the ones in which you deposit today your love and trust, for many of them will surely betray you, once you vibrate at a higher state.

"All that wish to live a godly life shall suffer persecution" (Timothy 3:12).

This is what I offer you, for it is the reason why I am here, and the reason why I have written so many books as the one you are reading now. For I have paid the same price too, when abdicating of the need to possess a house or a country, while traveling the world between several nations with nothing more than the essential.

Taking into consideration my need to feel loved, respected and appreciated, as well as my very social and outgoing nature, I cannot say that this journey has been any more than quite traumatic and extremely difficult at all levels for the past ten years. But I also know that it is transforming me into the leader the world needs, and not the one I wish I was or would like to be.

As a matter of fact, I do know that I would have more freedom to do many other things, in other fields, instead of sacrificing my entire time to writing, if the world was not near its end, and in need of my words, to make the final selection on who is supposed to be rescued from the final armageddon.

It would not be correct to tell you that I am superior to you, or your guru, but it is suitable to say to you that I am the way through the insanity of this world.

How to Embrace the Holy Truth

Reading my work is more than learning, for my writing possess more than knowledge; my writing style comes in code, and it is always written within a certain structure, based on sacred geometry. I will continue doing this, because I am just a messenger. I am not the ultimate truth, but merely a vehicle for that truth. And this awareness keeps me humble.

This is why I keep multiplying myself in different pen-names. I will keep doing this until this world has been shifted enough towards what I have come here to do.

I don't think anyone will notice me until I am long gone, although a few Freemasons, and Rosicrucians, especially the ones with nearly 90yo and beyond that, have clearly noticed my mission on Earth, and have treated me with the respect and consideration I have never seen before and anywhere else.

It is impressive how only a few can see what I am doing. But I guess even they needed over thirty to fifty years of spiritual work to be able to see me as me, and not as what I appear to be. The same applies to the Scientologists and many other groups and cults; although, I must admit, I also scare them with the amount of knowledge I possess. It is funny how they often say, "You are not supposed to know that until you are at the highest level".

Most of the individuals in the groups, religions and cults with the greatest amount of information and the most impressive private libraries, are so wise and, yet, so ignorant at the same time. For they read plenty but see very little.

One of their leaders even told me in private: "Every thousand of years, we have people coming to Earth to share their knowledge". And he was saying this to one of such individuals, even though I did not want to claim myself as such to him, or be perceived as either crazy or arrogant.

In these situations, I rather amuse myself by playing mind games: I describe how such people are and the challenges they face on Earth, to test and see the reactions.

It's funny how they say to everything, "Yes, it is true" and "Yes, they do that and experience that", agreeing with me on all the things I say regarding the biography of the messengers, and while not realizing I know it all so well because I am one of them too.

Humans are truly unbelievably impressive in how stupid they can be with so much knowledge. And yet, I am stuck here, as anybody else, doomed to the imbecility of having a nationality and a passport, and having to deal with behaviors I consider very inferior to my nature on a daily basis. I don't even know what to answer when someone asks me where I am from. They get confused when I say that I despise the people of the country where I was born. They think it's not normal to insult the people of your own nation.

Oh, humans! So very rooted on a prehistoric tribalistic mindset.

There is a long way ahead before humanity on Earth is able to transcend this stage of planetary evolution; and I often feel like I am trapped in prehistoric times considering everything I know. I end up trapped, between what I know, my spirit and my body.

The animalistic part of me wants more, and the spiritual part wants peace, and some times I just give up and take a nap, to handle the mental pressure. But traveling helps me in keeping myself motivated, and that's what I usually do, to protect my mental stability and keep myself focused on my work. Because the concept of nationality is a mental disease, as the idea that one possesses anything, including his or her own name; and so, there's no better way to escape such irrationality than to rebel against it, and enjoy life as God wanted for us, i.e., by loving the whole planet as one, and ourselves as a stream of abundance in constant transformation between the inside — our fluid personality — and the outside — the gifts of experience, when experienced freely and with gratitude, guided by the honest dreams emerging from within us.

This said, know that you can't evolve without the capacity to place yourself above the masses. For they are just zombies — with no idea about why they do what they do, or think and feel the way they experience these things.

SPIRITUAL WARFARE

Consciousness is reserved for a few only. Talking reason to the masses is like administrating medicine to the dead. And most books, because they are produced by the masses for the masses, are nothing more than dust in the wind. They will never amount to anything relevant over a period of a thousand or ten thousand years.

The real books you should be reading, are those who will change your soul, such as the ones I write. That is how you are able to realistically progress. And you will know that this is true, because, as Jesus said: "The truth will set you free". I.e., once you are free, you will see all the souls around you, trapped within their mind, their struggles and their spiritual wars, defeated and humiliated, self-absorbed in their emotional suffering. And only when you can recognize this on the masses, you will know that you are free. Only then, you will be able to see who is free, and why, and how few they are on a planet of billions.

This ability will necessarily make you an empath, and in doing so, help you recognize how the hierarchy of evil is formed on the planet and who is being enslaved by it, and by which values and beliefs.

This capacity to see things as they are, and not as they appear to be, will automatically shift your magnetic field, and start attracting different experiences towards you, which will then elevate you faster towards your new, and most high, true self.

How to Love Your Enemies

You don't need to love people as they appear to you. You can love the essence and the unseen potential in all souls. Know that they have lived many lives and are in the dark, unaware of their true self. This will make it easier for you to understand their struggles. Nonetheless, never ignore the threat they pose on you with their ignorance and lack of compassion. "One doesn't have to operate with great malice to do great harm. The absence of empathy and understanding are sufficient" (Charles M. Blow).

Throughout history, violent revolutions and mass oppression have been materialized, not for the reasons that appear to our mind, or the ones promoted by the education system, and in many cases, not even what was documented, but due to the lack of empathy and the vast amount of ignorance in the many.

The fact that most of the population still can't think for themselves, and numerous studies in psychology systematically prove us that almost anyone succumbs to peer pressure, and changes its values to match the majority, we continue to live in a world of idiots, where education did little to nothing to change the fact that we can annihilate ourselves at any moment, after being convinced of that by the media.

This, because "manipulating a group of people is easier than manipulating one person. For human society is like a nest of social insects. Buzz, buzz, buzz till suddenly the gang instinct kicks in and it is unanimous. Zoom, they swarm... So nobody wants to be caught dead near anybody the evil eye is on. Parents betray their children. Brothers betray sisters. Because people are like this, cynics can exploit and manipulate people like puppets. En-masse even. A sad fact but true" (Kathleen Krajco).

I have studied several martial arts, and taught many people too, including police officers; and I still get people, all the time, trying to bully me and intimidate me. And many times, I really do not know what to do, because real life is not like what the movies portray. And yet, I do know why people behave like this. You see, humans are weak creatures. Most people are constantly living in fear, especially men. I know this because I can feel it as I walk the streets of any country. And the way men deal with their fear, or even women, is by provoking someone else, who they think won't fight back. And so, sometimes, you see some pathetic creatures, shouting at you, as if they own the land, or consistently starring at you as you pass by, as if you had no right to be in the same place as them.

Even though such degrading and uncivilized behaviors, which we can see all over the world, are typically seen today in countries like the United States, Portugal, Spain and the Baltic nations, or even among tourists from Great Britain and the US visiting other nations, which is even more outrageous, for it permeates such pathetic fools with an aura of colonial arrogance, Lithuanians are specifically imbecile as a culture, and a perfect example to demonstrate this, namely, because they justify everything they do with the oppression they felt from the Soviet Union, and even though it is maintained nowadays only by their imaginary collective mind, feeding itself on the belief of an hypothetical enemy that actually doesn't exist anymore expect within them.

Now, I could tell you many stories about how I react, as in fact, martial arts have more to teach about the mind, than they do about fighting. Fighting, I would say, is the lowest level of training in any martial art. But the same principles apply to spirituality, as the material world is the first stage only on a transition to a higher stage.

Just as you change your reality with perceptions, you control your reality with perceptions too. And so, here are two real stories that happened to me, to explain you these contrasts better: One occurred in Lithuania; a woman was walking towards me with a cup of coffee in her hands. I had my own hands in the pockets and looked at her, as she looked back at me.

Now, at that point, I knew what she was doing as she is aware.

You see, Lithuanians like to play a "dare game" and especially women, in which they literally walk towards you to force you to move aside; it is childish, but what else to expect from a pathetic culture with pathetic people?

SPIRITUAL WARFARE

They act pathetically, like little children all the time, which is a typical behavior among those who demonstrate the lowest spiritual levels. "Age-old universal rule of courtesy does not apply to them. They exalt themselves at your expense. In their twisted thinking, falling short of the common standard of civility makes them feel superior. Because scoring an "F" makes one superior to someone who scores an "A", right?

We cannot help but sense, not only the put-down, but also the hostility in this behavior. So, it's unwise to go against our instincts and into denial about how this treatment makes us feel. It's the defense mechanism of a pathetic little people.

They acknowledge the existence of only their pets, people they have trained to wag their tails and mirror them. Everyone else is a threat to their flimsy facade.

The all-important word here is threat. They are hostile to anyone they view as a threat.

Ironically, when trying to control you, the same people may give you an impudent stare, maintaining an inappropriate eye contact in a kind of stare down. They do this on the premise that making others look bad makes them look good by comparison" (Kathleen Krajco).

In other words, because I have a strong energy and show confidence, I am constantly being provoked by those whose magnetic field shows the lowest vibratory levels.

Nevertheless, in this particular case, if she had coffee in her hands and saw me, and I am a man, who has more to lose, me or her?

You see, the interesting thing to notice here, as in what regards any engagement in conflicts with those who provoke them, is that those who do, naturally, and due to their own mental limitations, by the same rule, are also too unaware of their own weaknesses. And so, I continued to walk forward as she walked towards me; and as expected, I hit her shoulder and the coffee splashed on the floor.

As was also expected, she started shouting at me, like a little child who had just dropped the lollipop. And I continued to walk. And that's when she came behind me to stop me.

"Come see what you have done!", she childishly said, as if comparing a cup of coffee to a car crash; words that can make one only wonder if she would like to go to court over that and put me in jail for splashing her coffee on the floor. And on another hand, also words that portray clearly the level of immaturity and the state of irresponsibility she had, i.e., her neurosis.

There was no other way to answer such childish woman than to actually talk to her as if I was talking to a 5yo child.

"What have I done to you? Do tell me!", I asked calmly.

That's when I heard the unthinkable: "You pushed me and my coffee fell on the floor".

She had to formulate something that never happened to justify her insane behavior without any justification outside herself. And may this be a lesson to you about human beings, for they do this all the time when being irresponsible.

As I was dealing with, not only an immature person, but also someone clearly suffering from a mental illness, this time I replied her according to her mental status:

"How could I push you, if both of my hands were in my pockets? Actually, what really happened, is that I was walking calmly, with both of my hands inside the pockets of my jacket, as you see now, and you came towards me, and you dropped your own coffee by yourself; and, well, that's your problem, your fault, your responsibility; and not mine. You are a liar."

Upon hearing this, she literally froze, starring at me with her wide open psychotic eyes, like a dumb idiotic zombie. And that is when I walked away, while she remained unmoved, like a malfunctioning robot, remaining in the same place.

The greatest martial arts masters always said that the best fighters win without a fight, and here you have an example of that; I won with my hands inside the pockets of my jacket during the whole entire time.

SPIRITUAL WARFARE

Another similar situation occurred weeks later, in Poland. I was having breakfast with a friend who came to visit me for a weekend, and a waiter interrupted my conversation with her to take things from the table.

I was annoyed by his actions, looked at him and said: "You should to say, 'Excuse me' first, and not just interrupt people like that"; and he went into a psychotic rant, of blaming, creating excuses, justifying himself, and so on, circulating his words in all directions, as I watched him quietly and eventually started to smile at his madness.

He must have felt like his little ego had been hurt. And here we have again, another childlike scenario. Because, you see, most people, especially when they are rude, are actually being infantile and dramatizing their childhood.

That is why, I kept looking at him the whole time, and smiling as he was speaking, because I knew I was dealing with a child, not an adult.

Now, he was much taller than me, but I totally ignored that, as I wasn't afraid. And after his rant was over, he started apologizing repeatedly. And he apologized about seven times before he went away.

There have been other situations in my life, in which I shouted at people, and they reply like little children: "Why are you shouting at me?"

It's the same childlike trauma. Because you see, most people are mentally stuck in kindergarten. That is why they say I offend them when I force them to snap out of that mental state.

Such was the case of one of my friends, when I told her: "If I need to send you thirty messages explaining why you should respect me, maybe I am not dealing with a woman, and maybe you should join a kindergarten club to learn from fairytales what respect really is."

Again, and also in this situation, just like in the previous cases, she went into a psychotic rant, of blaming and justifications, before she finally started sending messages with smiley faces and asking why I am still talking to her.

It is basically the little child asking the adult: "Do you still love me after what I did?"

The Infantile Mind of Most Adults

Most people grow up only physically, into adult bodies, while thinking that love is granted. They don't want to deserve it. They never learned to deserve love. And then they wonder why all their relationships collapse.

I find it very hard to deal with the majority of the world, even though I travel a lot. Knowledge doesn't help me much, because, you see, there's no point in texting thirty messages to someone who feels no empathy, and can't understand love or respect. It is like talking Greek with a Mexican. People either see it or they don't. And that's why I tend to be more selective with whoever surrounds me and expansive towards meeting new people.

Nevertheless, I spend a lot of my time alone due to the obvious fact that most people are simply not adults, but little children in adult bodies, unable to rationalize normally or appreciate interactions in a healthy way.

This said, it's easy to love people when you don't feel remorse for talking reason, when you don't feel guilty for protecting your mental integrity and personal values, and when you can acknowledge that they are not truly aware of themselves, or capable of understanding social interactions in a mature level, but purely egotistical, like a small child thinking that the sun and the stars exist only to satisfy his or her needs.

It doesn't mean that you are loving them for what they show you, or loving them for the potential beneath their level of consciousness, but that you, yourself, are coming from a place of love and abundance.

Once you can do that, you won't fear antagonistic situations, and you won't hate others, but merely be aware. Because there is a big difference between hating people and hating their actions, hating a situation or hating yourself by how you react to it, resenting a moment in life or letting it go and fadeaway as just another memory of your past.

The greatest difference in all these cases, is that you are able to continue loving yourself; and if you can do that, you can send love to others from the distance, you can pray for them, and you can even continue in sharing your love with those who are ready to receive it.

On the other hand, if you allow the negative energy of others to possess your spirit, you will start hating yourself, resenting yourself; and once this occurs, you can't love anyone else. For you will be in a state of hate yourself.

Don't fool yourself into thinking that you can love without sanity. Sanity always comes first. As a matter of fact, "trying to drive a person insane is just a way of murdering them. When you do that to a person, you kill that person just as surely as if you shot them dead. And you do it more cruelly than if you shot them dead" (Kathy Krajco).

This is why I mentioned the topic of martial arts, as even if your ultimate purpose is to win without a fight, you may need to fight to protect your integrity, and you shouldn't be hold by fear when that moment comes.

Unfortunately, the truth is that, when someone is testing your boundaries, that person, soon enough, will start stepping into your comfort zone, in order to attack your mental stability, your sanity; and if he or she succeeds, the next stage is physical violence.

Quite often, these things, these stages as I described them, do occur and manifest themselves within minutes. Because the absence of a response in such situations — that most people tend to assume to be the most ideal behavior — actually ends up being perceived as weakness by the perpetrator, therefore stimulating the engagement towards the next stage of violence.

When that happens, many of us, succumb to fear. Because "fear is a state of imperception, fear is an unwillingness to confront. If one cannot confront, he cannot become aware of. So, if one is unwilling to confront, then he doesn't know what he is confronting and he doesn't see what is in front of him and he can dream up this mirage called 'the viciousness of Man.'" (L. Ron Hubbard).

SPIRITUAL WARFARE

It is the unwillingness to confront our problems that makes us insane and negative towards ourselves and the rest of the world.

How to Protect Your Soul

This world, as it is, doesn't present us many options, if we wish to maintain our sanity.

In my personal case, and as a writer of so many books, sanity is my Holy Grail. My mind has to be in perfect shape, for me to work so much and so clearly and so fast, from Monday to Sunday, or I fall into a depression; or worse, as in being terribly sick, and laying down in bed for several days, as was the case before, when I was teaching college students and having my vital energy drained out of my body in every class. It would take me an average of three days to recover from that.

Fortunately, I was only working an average of three days a week, reason why I was able to endure such situation for a couple of years, before deciding to become a full-time author and start a few companies of my own, to make a living without needing a job anymore.

Obviously, it's hard to be an adult in a world of little children in grown up bodies, leveling themselves during the day by draining the energy of others. But that's what it is, that's what we are faced with on this planet.

Most people have not truly grown up, and their awareness level is extremely limited. So don't blame yourself for what happens around you. Even though it affects your self-esteem, you shouldn't blame yourself for what you do or don't do. In the end, your sanity is what matters the most.

Always focus on visualizations and in loving yourself, and let the world be what it is; for you can't fight it alone, but only be yourself as you are, and protect your most precious asset — your sanity, or to be more precise, your overall health and energy frequency.

Whenever you need to confront provocations, remember that you are dealing with a child, and not an adult. Truly mature people don't need to compete with anyone, for they are obsessed with their dreams and in love with their self-improvement as a spiritual being.

This planet has laws that can be seen in our interactions. But remember that I said previously that most people are not aware of why they feel and think the way they do, and try to justify their behavior to deny consciousness; and the less spiritual they are, the more likely they will do this, and the more self-absorbed they are within themselves, not truly seeing the counter-effects of their actions.

It's a strange thing, until you understand it by comparing with the state of self-hypnosis. Because it is, indeed, as if everyone was hypnotized into thinking that they are just chickens and their actions, controlled by the one hypnotizing them, perfectly justifiable.

I ask you to simply observe how easily people are hypnotized by a professional and led into thinking that they are someone whom they are not, to understand the state of mankind, for it is indeed a state of mass hypnosis.

This said, imagine only what a greater expert in hypnosis, such as a demon, with thousand of years of experience in dealing with human weaknesses, could do. For what he could, surely is.

The Deception in Atheism

Atheists and agnostics tend to be extremely neurotic and psychotic, due precisely to the spiritual laws that govern them, either they are aware of it or not, either they believe in them or not.

They are more easily put in a trance than anyone else. And therefore, are more easily controlled by mass opinion and the media as well.

What this means is that, the physical aspect of reality, is merely the superficial manifestation of laws, that can indeed be studied at a Quantum Level.

It is known, for example, that the higher the state of vibrational energy of a being, the more it attracts its opposite, trying to nullify it. And so, we can also say that not all laws are necessarily good at an individual level. This one, for example, shows us that we need to evolve as a collective; it exist to deny contradictions on the same plane.

In other words, one needs to adjust his state by expanding, and not allowing himself to be suppressed.

There are three ways to expand yourself:

- Physical, through demonstrated power, which also leads to a reinforced vibratory energy, often manifested in groups, congregations and communities;

- Mental, with knowledge and strategy, namely, with the planning and better organization of your time;

- Emotional, through the heart, and which gains the most impact with visualizations, with the knowing that you are much more and greater than your own experiences.

The combined force of these three elements is relatively easy to apply if you discard your egotistical needs and put them aside.

For example, I usually work in the morning, in order to avoid the masses at the end of the day, as their concentrated energy has more impact on me, as when contrasted with the energy and thoughts of one or two individuals during the morning, which I can easily nullify by simply being present, in my own vibrational state.

Once my emotions are at balance, I don't require much from the mental and physical planes. And yet, my mental activity is constant during the whole time I am awaken, due to the fact I am always either writing, researching or simply reading.

As for the physical energy, it comes from all the groups I am associated with, and I certainly need them more when under a collective spiritual attack, which occurs regularly, as when the individuals I know become possessed.

The Importance of Prayer

Because the Devil can't get to me directly, it has been common, through all of my existence, to see those around me becoming possessed. It is how I am attacked — through the ones I trust the most, and indirectly.

Now, we all become weaker under constant pressure. And so, you should keep this in mind, in order to protect your vibration.

Not many people recover quickly after strong attacks on their self-esteem and physical energy. Many develop illnesses and die. And this is something you should be aware at all moments.

In fact, a demonic attack on a very elevated spirit doesn't come at once, but consistently, in small doses, until this individual is too weak to fightback on his own.

Many of the governmental laws of the modern world, also tend to be more effective in protecting aggressors rather than victims. Besides, a psychic assault or verbal insult is never something you can easily justify in any court of today's world, even though it can be more devastating on your mental health than anything else.

You can only protect yourself of such incidents by moving away from the many and joining the few. "Walk away from the 97% and join the 3%. Don't go where they go; don't do what they do; don't talk like they talk. Develop your own language and be part of the few" (Jim Rohn). "In times of war, as in life, surround yourself with people of value, virtue and high morals, because it's always better to lose, perish and vanish in glory than to live in shame" (Robin Sacredfire).

In your darkest moments, when you feel that you are alone and without hope, simply pray, for strength and answers.

A prayer should be repeated every morning and every night, in order to reinforce your aura and enable your mind with more clarity.

You can choose to read all the prayers presented in this book, or choose one to memorize and use frequently. All and each one of them follows a specific pattern, either related to symbols or chakras.

Once you are able to memorize it, please repeat the prayer with your eyes closed, while sitting on a comfortable position with your hands on top of your heart. And make sure that you feel the words as you speak them, for the power of these prayers comes fundamentally from your emotions and capacity to visualize the meanings behind the words.

The Prayer of the Cross

I forgive myself for my past,

as I place my attention in my future,

with faith in God,

and faith in myself;

For just as I was able to achieve happiness before,

I can also and will certainly feel happiness again;

With the belief that I can and will

attract more wealth and love

as much as I work towards my own wisdom,

while accumulating life experiences.

The Prayer of the Pentagram

With God as my friend

and my trust in God

I shall attract good thoughts and ideas;

for as much as I love the world,

and attract this love unto my life,

I become a better person.

And I'll always trust God for guidance,

towards seeing the best in others,

as much as they show me

whom God wants me to love;

because I can and will always see love,

while attracting it to my life,

and in doing so,

grow as a loving person.

The Prayer to the God of the Invisible World

God of the invisible world,

bring today my daily wisdom,

and let me speak only what is good,

as I feel it within my heart;

and guide me towards my best experiences,

as I allow myself to be guided with love,

and let me not fall into guilt, shame,

regret, remorse or resentment,

but enlighten me through what the world offers.

The Prayer of the Chakras

I now let go of all my fears, from past and present,

while recognizing that I'm bigger than what is ahead of me,

and can overcome everything that makes me scared.

If I fail along the journey of my life,

I shall not let guilt consume me

or repent for anything I do,

but forgive myself for what I did wrong.

I accept all aspects of myself,

and I don't let shame live inside me,

but instead replace it with love for myself,

and the acceptance of my true nature.

In doing so, I release all fears within me,

and let go of the pain and sadness related to my past,

while blessing everyone who has been with me.

I am ready to accept the truth within me,

and in doing so, I refuse to lie about my true self,

just as much as I refuse to accept the lies of others.

I will not let the illusions of this world fool me,

but instead receive insights from such world,

and through this world, attract wisdom towards me,

knowing that everything and everyone is connected.

As I recognize and let go of all my attachments,

I also embrace the cosmic energy of the universe in me,

and allow it to fulfill me and fill me with infinite love.

In doing so, I surrender myself to God and the Highest Truth,

and embrace what is pure and beautiful in my existence,

within my real self and my spirit,

my eternal soul and its consciousness;

For I am one with the Creation,

and one with the Universe.

The Prayer of Hope

I let go of my fears,

because I have faith in my future;

and if I fail, I shall learn, and forgive myself,

for I am not ashamed of wanting happiness;

and I deserve to be happy as I am,

while letting go of the sadness within me,

because it made me who I am today;

And so, I bless those who guided me

and made me who I am now,

as much as I accept my true nature;

And I shall not be fooled by illusions,

but obtain insights from the world,

while loving knowledge and wisdom,

seeing that everything is connected;

For this truth sets me free from attachments

to things, people and even my emotions,

while connecting me to the cosmic energy

and the universe that manifests it within me;

For I am one with God and the Truth,

and accept what is eternal and beautiful;

And I seek to gain a higher consciousness,

while attracting to my life that which is good,

by manifesting what I dream and desire.

The Prayer of Good Fortune

If this book helped you achieve a better state of mind and more enlightenment, share the love with the world by using the following prayer to improve your level of empathy.

Choose one person, either someone you love, someone you care about, someone who hurt you, or even the author of this book, and repeat the following prayer.

God of the Universe,

bring today the daily wisdom that... (his/her name), needs,

and guide him/her towards only what is good,

as they feel these words within their heart;

and take them towards their best experiences,

as they allow themselves to be guided with love,

while releasing them from guilt, shame,

regret, remorse and resentment;

and may they be enlightened

through what the world can offer them.

The Prayer for Exorcism

If you wish to use a prayer to help a lost soul from the distance, please repeat the following one with the image of such person in your mind or by using a photo for guidance.

You must repeat the prayer, word by word, for it is the same practiced by Vatican priests.

If you wish to access more information about it, please consult the manuals of Malachi Martin or another well-known professional exorcist.

You can also use the same prayer on yourself.

Do not remember, O Lord, our sins

or those of our forefathers,

and do not punish us for our offenses.

And lead us not into temptation,

but deliver us from evil.

Save this man/woman, your servant,

because he/she hopes in you, My God.

Be a tower of strength for him/her, O Lord,

in the face of the Enemy.

Let the enemy have no victory over him/her,

and let the Son of Iniquity not succeed in injuring him/her.

Send him/her Heavenly protection.

Lord, hear my prayer,

and let my cry reach you.

May the Lord be with you,

and with your spirit.

The Prayer for Soul Liberation

Hear our prayer, so that this servant of yours

who is bound with the chain of sins,

be mercifully freed by the compassion of your goodness.

Holy Lord! All-powerful Father! Eternal God!

Father of Our Lord Jesus Christ!

You who destined that recalcitrant

and apostate Tyrant to the fires of Hell;

You who sent Your only son into this world

in order that he might crush this Roaring Lion:

Look speedily and snatch from damnation

and from this Devil of our times this man/woman

who was created in your image and likeness.

Throw your terror, Lord, over the Beast

who is destroying what belongs to you.

Give faith to your servants against this most Evil Serpent,

to fight most bravely.

So that the Serpent not hold in contempt those who hope in you,

and say - as It said through the Pharaoh: I do not know God,

and I will not let Israel go.

Let your powerful strength force the Serpent to let go of your servant, so that it no longer possess him/her

whom you deigned to make in your image

and to redeem by your son,

Who lives and reigns with you

in the unity of the Holy Spirit, as God,

for ever and ever.

Amen!

The Prayer of St. Michael

St. Michael, the Archangel,

illustrious leader of the heavenly army,

defend us in the battle

against principalities and powers,

against the rulers of the world of darkness

and the spirit of wickedness in high places.

Come to the rescue of mankind,

whom God has made in His own image and likeness,

and purchased from Satan's tyranny at so great a price.

Holy Church venerates you as her patron and guardian.

The Lord has entrusted to you the task

of leading the souls of the redeemed

to heavenly blessedness.

Entreat the Lord of peace to cast Satan

down under our feet,

so as to keep him from further holding man captive

and doing harm to the Church.

Carry our prayers up to God's throne,

that the mercy of the Lord may quickly come

and lay hold of the beast, the serpent of old,

DAN DESMARQUES

Satan and his demons,

casting him in chains into the abyss,

so that he can no longer seduce the nations.

About the Publisher

This book was published by the 22 Lions Bookstore.
For more books like this visit www.22Lions.com.
Join us on social media at:
Fb.com/22Lions;
Twitter.com/22lionsbookshop;
Instagram.com/22lionsbookshop;
Pinterest.com/22LionsBookshop.

www.ingramcontent.com/pod-product-compliance
Lightning Source LLC
Chambersburg PA
CBHW050443010526
44118CB00013B/1653